Anonymus

The Standard Guide to Knitting

According to the new Code

Anonymus

The Standard Guide to Knitting
According to the new Code

ISBN/EAN: 9783742831415

Manufactured in Europe, USA, Canada, Australia, Japa

Cover: Foto ©Thomas Meinert / pixelio.de

Manufactured and distributed by brebook publishing software
(www.brebook.com)

Anonymus

The Standard Guide to Knitting

THE STANDARD GUIDE

TO

KNITTING

ACCORDING TO THE NEW CODE

BY

A LADY MANAGER

———————

DEDICATED BY PERMISSION TO

H.R.H. THE PRINCESS LOUISE

(MARCHIONESS OF LORNE)

———————

SECOND EDITION

LONDON

EDWARD STANFORD, 55 CHARING CROSS, S.W.

SOLD AT NATIONAL SOCIETY'S DEPÔT, WESTMINSTER

CONTENTS.

NEEDLEWORK.

THE following circular to Her Majesty's inspectors, on the subject of Needlework, has been issued from the Education Department, dated April 30, 1879 :—

SIR,—As the time is at hand when the provisions of the Code as to the examination of needlework in public elementary schools will take effect, I am directed to offer some suggestions for your guidance in this particular.

1. The children should be arranged for the examination, according to their ability in this branch of their work, in 'divisions' and 'stages' following the order shown in Schedule III. As each child should be presented in the highest 'stage' of which she is able to do the necessary work (Rules 1 and 4), it is evident that these 'stages' will not usually correspond with the 'standards' (Article 28). You will often find it useful to require that the change of organisation from ordinary classes to needlework 'stages' should be made during your inspection and in your presence. This will afford you an opportunity of estimating the discipline of a school from a special point of view, and will also enable you to see at a glance how far the children are familiar with and interested in their separate organisations for needlework.

2. Care must be taken to ensure that a fair proportion of children is presented in the upper stages, as the work of those becomes imperative (Rule 5). In several districts children of nine years of age are already being presented in work equivalent to that of Stage IV.; my lords, therefore, trust that if your district is not yet in a position to produce similar results, you will lose no time in urging on the managers and teachers the importance of realising them.

3. You will have observed that Rule 6 recommends, though it

does not positively require, that infant boys should be taught according to its provisions. This is being accomplished by some of your colleagues with excellent effect, and my lords wish you to take every opportunity of encouraging the practice. It is found that boys so taught quickly improve in general handiness and precision.

4. When (as is frequently the case) children over seven are retained in an infant school, a correspondingly larger proportion of the whole number of scholars should be presented in the 'upper division'; the children over seven should, as a rule, show greater proficiency in the work of that division, and those parts of it which had previously been optional should then, for girls at all events, cease to be so regarded.

5. My lords think that from forty-five to sixty minutes should be devoted to these needlework exercises. Whether the examination should or should not be simultaneous throughout the school must be left to your discretion. If you decide upon setting all the children to work at once, you can employ your own time in examining the specimen garments produced, in verifying registers, hearing pupil-teachers read and repeat, &c. ; and in mixed schools in the examination of the boys in their corresponding subject under Article 19, c. 1; provided always that such employment does not unduly interfere with the due supervision of the needlework examination by yourself or your assistant.

6. It would scarcely be possible, even in an hour's examination, to test each girl in every part of the work taught in each stage (especially in the upper stages); you will probably find it convenient to subdivide each stage or division into two or more groups, to each of which distinct kinds of work should be assigned.

The following examples are put forth suggestively; but it must be left to your discretion to adopt them, whether wholly or in part, according to the special circumstances of each case. You should, therefore, be careful that no girl knows beforehand what precise exercise she will individually be called upon to perform.

STAGE I.—Group 1.—*To *fix* and work a hem about 5 inches long.

Group 2.—*To *fix* and work a counter-hem about 3 inches long.

STAGE II.—Group 1.—*To *fix* and work 3 or 4 inches of seaming and felling.

Group 2.—*To *fix* and hem a square corner, and tack 3 or 4 pleats.

STAGE III.—Group 1.—*To *fix* and work 3 inches of stitching, and to sew on a string.

Group 2.—To darn as for a thin place about 12 rows on moderately fine canvas, and to mark one of her own initials.

Group 3.—*To *fix* and hem a square corner, and herring-bone about 3 inches.

STAGE IV.—Group 1.—To do about 6 inches of gathering, to stroke it down and set it into a band, and to sew on a string.

Group 2.—To work a button-hole, one end round, the other square, to sew on a linen button (not pierced), and to darn as if for a thin place about 20 rows 1 inch long on stocking material.

Group 3.—To herring-bone about 6 inches on flannel, and to mark 2 initials of own name on coarse material.

Group 4.—To set in a patch (2 inches square) in calico.

STAGE V.—Group 1.—To turn down and tack a hem ¾ inch wide; on this work a button-hole, and run two tucks about 4 inches long above it.

Group 2.—To set in a flannel patch (2 inches square).

Group 3.—To hem, whip, and set on a frill about 4 inches long.

Group 4.—To plain-darn a hole in stocking material, and mark on coarse material any two letters.

Group 5.—To cut out and tack together the pattern of a girl's shift or pinafore, *or the pattern of the garment she has made for the inspection.*

---

* The fixing in Stages I., II., and III. is optional (Rule 8).

STAGE VI.—Group 1.—To darn a thin place (Swiss darning), and to graft 3 inches.

Group 2.—To set in a flannel patch (2 inches square).

Group 3.—To darn a diagonal cut, and to mark any two letters on fine calico.

Group 4.—To cut out in paper and tack together the body of a baby's frock, *or the pattern of the garment she has made for the inspection.*

You will have noticed that knitting is not included in the above specimen groups. This subject may perhaps be conveniently judged by the specimens produced for inspection; but it may be advisable, occasionally, to question the children orally, or to make a few of them do some of this work in your presence, so as to satisfy you of their expertness.

The managers should provide, before the day of inspection, and have ready for distribution, suitable pieces of material, according to the different 'divisions' and 'stages,' together with a full supply of needles, cottons, *scissors*, thimbles, &c., and paper (newspaper or ruled to show selvedge) for cutting out. Each child should also have a label showing her name, age, and the stage in which she is presented, which she must affix to her work when finished, after securely fastening together the different pieces of her work, if she has used more than one.

In large schools you may sometimes find it necessary to select girls from each 'stage,' instead of examining all who are presented under Article 19, c. 1.

This will, no doubt, save time, as the rest of the children can meanwhile be examined in some other subject, but you must bear in mind that in such cases it will be more difficult to determine whether a creditable examination has been passed (Article 19, c. 4). It will be advisable, therefore, not to have recourse to this method except in cases of emergency, or where, from your previous knowledge of the school, you have good reason to know that the subject is well and evenly taught.

7. My lords attach great importance to the cutting out and making of garments. You will therefore inquire whether the

former is regularly taught, and on what system, and will as often as possible call upon a fair proportion of girls in Stages V. and VI. to cut out paper patterns in your presence. You will also require from every girl qualified for examination under Article 19, c. 2, a garment or similar piece of work (certified to have been done by herself) exhibiting the various stitches to be learnt in the stage in which she is being presented. In and above Stage IV. such garment must have been cut out by the child herself.

In the case of half-timers one garment may be the work of two girls. In infant schools, and in others where children are not presented in needlework under Article 19, c. 1, but only under Article 17 £, you may, at your discretion, test their proficiency by specimens worked in your presence, but you will not be able to report favourably of a school in which each scholar in Stages III. and IV. of a girls' school does not produce a garment or other complete piece of work; and, in future years, this condition will be expected to be satisfied in the case of infants in the upper division (Article 19 A. (1), note).

From information received from time to time from several of your colleagues, my lords know that many schools are already carrying out the requirements of Schedule III.; and that others, having now had these requirements before them for a twelvemonth, are prepared to meet them. Where, however, such is not yet the case, you will, during the present year, show great leniency, especially where you see reason to believe that such encouragement will accomplish the desired end. In no case, however, must the grant (Article 19, c. 1) be recommended for bad or careless work; but where you find that the children, although not yet able to fulfil, in all particulars, the requirements of the Code, are being well grounded, and that a good system of instruction is being pursued, you will recommend the payment, being, however, careful to point out to managers and teachers that such leniency is not to be expected in future.

I am, Sir,

Your obedient Servant,

F. R. SANDFORD.

P.S.—It may be convenient that some such materials as the following should be provided ready for distribution, on the day of inspection, to each girl who is presented under Art. 19, c. 2:—

STAGE I.—A strip of white or unbleached calico 7 inches by 3. For those who are called upon to do counter-hemming, these will be divided so as to form two pieces.

STAGE II.—A piece of white or unbleached calico 4 inches square. For those who are called upon to do seaming and felling, these will be divided so as to form two pieces 4 inches by 2 inches.

STAGE III.—A piece of brown holland, about 4 inches square, pieces of tape about 2 inches long, canvas for darning and marking, and flannel for herring-boning.

STAGE IV.—A piece of brown holland, of coarse though thin linen, or of calico, about 5 inches square, linen buttons not pierced, pieces of stocking material (coarse) for darning, and flannel for herring-boning.

STAGES V. and VI.—Same as for Stage IV., only of finer material, and with the addition of cambric or mull muslin for frills, and of paper (newspaper or ruled to show selvedge) for cutting out.

In addition to this every girl must have thimble, needle, suitable cotton, and (in the upper stages) scissors. She should also have a label showing her name, age, and the stage in which presented, which she must affix to her work, when finished, first fastening together securely her different pieces if she has worked on more than one. Knitting-needles and wool or cotton (according to the stage) should be in readiness, in case Her Majesty's inspector should desire them.

INTRODUCTORY REMARKS

ON

KNITTING.

***

THE personal instruction and assistance of a good teacher are necessary, for a child to learn the rudiments of knitting.

Knitting Cotton

should be used to teach knitting; wool is apt to split. Strutt's unbleached knitting cotton will make very strong stockings, but is not so attractive to children as coloured yarn. Scarlet wool is suitable for cuffs, but is not strong enough for stockings. Violet, grey, and brown wools are suitable for stockings; they are strong and wash well. Blue and crimson wools do not wash well.

As some children knit loosely and others knit tightly, it is better to measure the inches than to count the rows of knitting.

In measuring knitting, the work should

be placed on the table, and the measure
laid fairly on it to count the inches.

A stocking of any size can be knitted by
measuring the number of inches of the
leg, foot, &c., of a pattern stocking. The
measures should be written down, and the
stocking should be knitted to the exact size.

The heels and toes of stockings can be
made strong by knitting with double wool,
or from a second ball of wool of the same
colour as the stocking, of a finer quality.

If the stocking be of grey wool, Taylor's
white Persian thread No. 3, may be
knitted with wool for the heel and toe ;
this will strengthen the stocking without
making it clumsy.

A ridge in plain knitting consists of two
rows of knitting.

Scotch yarn, and needles No. 14, will
make an elastic but not a fine stocking.

To knit evenly is the result of practice ;
it is difficult at first to knit two stockings of exactly the same size, even if
they have the same number of stitches
and rows.

Twenty Rules for Knitting Socks and Stockings.

1. *Are there any rules about beginning to knit socks or stockings?*

The rules about beginning to knit socks and stockings are—The knitting should be cast on rather loosely ; the end of wool or cotton should be knitted into the first six stitches ; the knitter's hands should be freshly washed, and an inch measure should be at hand ; the knitter should not talk while knitting.

2. *Is there any rule in knitting with two needles?*

In knitting with two needles, slip the first stitch of each row without knitting it.

3. *Is there any rule in knitting with four needles?*

In knitting with four needles, knit the first stitch of each needle tightly, or a line will be seen at the change of needles.

4. *When fresh wool or cotton is required, how is it joined to the knitting?*

When fresh wool or cotton is required, lay six inches of the end of the fresh wool or cotton over six inches of the other end *reversed*, knit six stitches with the two ends of wool or cotton together.

5. *Is there any rule about ribbing socks or stockings?*

. The best ribbing for socks and stockings is, knit 2, purl 2 ; therefore the number of stitches should be any number of fours, 48, 52, 56, 60, 64, 68, 72, 76, 80, 92, and so on.   Stockings require two inches of ribbing ; socks require three inches of ribbing.

6. *In how many places are socks and stockings decreased?*

Children's socks are decreased in three places, the heel, the instep, and the toe. Stockings are decreased in four places, the leg, the heel, the instep, and the toe. Gentlemen's socks should be decreased in the leg.

7. *Is there any rule about the number of stitches for the feet of stockings?*

The rule about the number of stitches for the feet of stockings is, that the number of stitches for the foot after the instep decreasings *must* be the same as the number of stitches for the ankle after the leg decreasings.

8. *How are the stitches of small socks placed after the ribbing?*

After the ribbing of small socks place the right number of stitches on the heel needle at once, an equal number on each side of the seam stitch. The stitches for the instep should be one or two more in number than the stitches for the heel. In a sock of 48 stitches, take 25 for the instep and 23 for the heel; 11 stitches on each side of the seam stitch.

9. *How are the stitches of stockings placed after the ribbing?*

After the ribbing of stockings, place the titches as equally in number as possible on

B

the three needles. In a stocking of 68 stitches, place 23 stitches on the first needle, 11 stitches on each side of the seam stitch ; 23 stitches on the second needle ; and 22 stitches on the third needle.

10. *How are decreasings marked?*

Decreasings may be marked thus, to assist counting the rows: Thread a needle with white cotton, double loop the cotton through the first decreasing of each decreasing row until the sock or stocking is finished.

11. *How is every 3rd stitch increased along the heel of socks or stockings.*

The increased stitch is made by knitting a stitch into the loop at the back of the stitch as well as knitting a stitch into the stitch itself.

12. *Are there any rules about putting away stocking knitting.*

In putting away stocking knitting, finish the row or needle; draw the stitches together, give the knitting a slight pull lengthways, wind up the wool or cotton ; with the spare needle, pin the knitting to the ball of wool or cotton.

13. *What are the best needles for knitting stockings?*

Steel knitting needles of the best quality, 6 inches long, should be used for knitting stockings.

14. *Which is the best wool for knitting stockings?*

Scotch Fingering Yarn is best for girls' or women's stockings. Irish yarn is very strong and thick, fit for boys' or men's stockings. Welsh Yarn is fit for the first size sock.

15. *How should stockings be finished?*

Stockings should be cast off on the outside. The end of wool should be darned into the knitting.

16. *Is there any way of making stockings very strong?*

To make stockings very strong, from the

beginning of the heel and from the first decreasing of the toe, knit with double yarn—that is, from two balls of yarn at once—to the end of the heel and toe.

17. *How is the seam of stockings made?*

The seam stitch may be purled in every row or in every other row.

18. *Describe the Carlisle toe of stockings.*

The Carlisle toe is decreased very gradually until only one stitch remains. It is knitted thus: Divide the foot into any number of sevens, knit 5 stitches knit 2 together all round, knit 5 plain rounds. Knit 4 stitches knit 2 together all round, knit 4 plain rounds. Knit 3 stitches knit 2 together all round, knit 3 plain rounds. Knit 2 stitches knit 2 together all round, knit 2 plain rounds. Knit one stitch knit 2 together all round, knit 1 plain round. Knit 2 together all round till only 1 stitch remains. Cast off, and secure the end of yarn into the knitting.

19. *Can stockings of any size be ribbed?*

A stocking cast on with any number of
fours may be ribbed thus: Knit 2, purl 2 ;
or knit 1, purl 1. Omit the seam stitch,
knit the heel, the sole of the foot, and the
toe plain.

20. *Are the heels of stockings easy to knit?*

The square heel of woven stockings
described in the ' Annie Stocking ' is very
easy to knit. There are many other heels,
such as the following:—

The Margaret Heel.

After the straight part of the heel is
knitted omit the seam stitch, mark the
middle of the row, knit to the middle of
the row, knit 2, knit 2 together, knit 1.
Turn back. Purl to the middle of the
row, purl 2, purl 2 together, purl 1.
Repeat to the end of the heel. Take up
the side stitches, as in the square heel.

The Louisa Heel.

Knit to the middle of the row, knit 3, knit 2 together, knit 1. Turn back. Purl to the middle of the row, purl 3, purl 2 together, purl 1. Repeat to the end of the heel.

The Sarah Heel

SMALL SOCK.

Knit to the middle of the row, knit 2, slip 1, knit 1, cross the slip stitch over it. Turn back. Purl to the middle of the row, purl 2, purl 2 together. Repeat to the end of the heel.

LARGE SOCK.

Knit to the middle of the row, knit 4, slip 1, knit 1, cross the slip stitch over it. Turn back. Purl to the middle of the row, purl 4, purl 2 together. Repeat.

INFANTS' DEPARTMENT.

LOWER DIVISION.
UPPER DIVISION.

GIRLS' DEPARTMENT.

FIRST STAGE.

For children who have not been in an
Infants' Department.

Knitting—2 needles. A strip, 3 inches
by 18 inches, with cotton.

CHAIN EDGE.

Knitting Cotton No. 8.   Two Needles No. 14.

Cast on 24 stitches.

Knit 120 ridges.

Cast off.

To form a chain at each edge of the
knitting, place the right hand needle
through the first stitch of the left hand
needle as if for purling, draw the stitch

on to the right hand needle ; the cotton which is above the stitch place at the back of it ; knit the rest plain. This chain edge should be made in all plain knitting.

Use.

Six of the above strips can be sewn together to make a duster. 18 strips will make a bath towel. They can also be used for learning the darning stitch.

In sewing the strips together use knitting cotton and a large darning needle. Tack the strips together first ; get the ridges opposite each other. Be very careful to sew both strips one stitch from the edge. Fasten on and off securely, and darn the end of cotton into the knitting.

GIRLS' DEPARTMENT.

SECOND STAGE.

For children who have not passed the Upper Division in Infants' Department.

Knitting—2 needles. Plain and purled rows alternately. A strip as above. Four needles. Wristlets or muffatees.

CHAIN EDGE.

Knitting Cotton No. 8.   Two Needles No. 14.

Cast on 24 stitches.

1st Row.—Chain edge the first stitch knit three stitches plain, purl 16 stitches, knit 4 stitches plain.

2nd Row.—Knit plain. Repeat these 2 rows till there are 120 ridges in the border. Cast off.

Use.

FOR A LAMP DUSTER OF THE TWO STRIPS.

Knit together 7 strips: the 1, 3, 5, 7 of plain knitting; the 2, 4, 6 of plain and purl knitting.

FOR A BATH TOWEL.

Knit together 15 strips: the 1, 3, 5, 7, 9, 11, 13, 15 of plain knitting; the 2, 4, 6, 8, 10, 12, 14 of plain and purl knitting.

WRISTLETS OR MUFFATEES.

(Lady's.)

Single Berlin Wool. Four Needles No. 14.

Cast on 44 stitches. Knit 2, purl 2, for 5½ inches. Cast off. Darn the end of wool into the knitting.

(Gentleman's.)

Cast on 48 stitches. Knit 2, purl 2, for 6 inches. Cast off. Darn the end of wool into the knitting.

THIRD STAGE.

Knitting—4 needles.   Plain and purled
alternately.   Socks.

THE HAMILTON RIBBED SOCK.

Scotch yarn, 4 Needles No. 14.

Leg 40 stitches.   Knit 3 inches.
Heel 20 stitches.   Knit 2 inches.
Foot 40 stitches.   Knit 3 inches.

Decrease in 4 rounds of the toe.
Cast off with 24 stitches.

Ribbing.

40 Stitches.

Cast on 40 stitches.
Knit 2, purl 2, for 3 inches (30 rounds).

Leg.

40 *Stitches.*

Knit 1, purl 1, for 3 inches (30 rounds).

Heel.

20 *Stitches.*

Do not continue the ribbing ; knit in rows plain and purl. Slip the 1st stitch of each row. Knit 2 inches (20 rows).

Mark the middle of the heel with a loop of white cotton.

1st Row.—Knit to the middle of the row, knit 2, knit 2 together, knit 1. Turn back.

2nd Row.—Purl to the middle of the row, purl 2, purl 2 together, purl 1.

Repeat these 2 rows till the heel is finished.

Instep.

20 *Stitches.*

Take up 16 stitches on each side of the heel. Place the 20 instep stitches on one needle, knit the 2 heel needles plain, and rib the instep needle for 1 round. Mark each decreasing of the 1st heel needle with a loop of white cotton. Decrease thus :— 1st heel needle, knit plain till 4 stitches are left, knit 2 together, knit 2. Instep needle, rib. 2nd heel needle, knit 1, slip 1, knit 1, cross the slip stitch over the last knitted stitch, knit the rest plain. Knit 1 round without decreasing between each decreasing round. Decrease till there are 40 stitches on the 3 needles.

Foot.

40 *Stitches.*

Rib the upper needle. Knit the 2 under needles plain for 3 inches (30 rounds). Measure from the join of the heel.

Toe.

40 *Stitches.*

Begin with the upper needle. Knit the whole of the toe plain. Mark each 1st decreasing of the upper needle with a loop of white cotton. Decrease thus :—Knit

2, slip 1, knit 1, cross the slip stitch over the last knitted stitch, knit plain till 4 stitches are left on the needle, slip 1, knit 1, cross the slip stitch over the last knitted stitch, knit 2.

1st under needle, knit 2, slip 1, knit 1, cross the slip stitch over the last knitted stitch, knit the rest plain. 2nd under needle, knit plain till 4 stitches are left on the needle, slip 1, knit 1, cross the slip stitch over the last knitted stitch, knit 2. Knit 2 plain rounds between each decreasing round. After the 4th decreasing round place the 12 under stitches on one needle. Cast off from both needles at once on the right side. Darn the end of yarn into the knitting.

FOURTH STAGE.

Knitting—4 needles.   A full-sized Youth's
Sook.

THE ERNEST SOCK.

Scotch Yarn.   4 Needles No. 14.

Leg 56 stitches.   Knit 6 inches.
Ankle 50 stitches.   Knit 1 inch.
Heel 25 stitches.   Knit 2 inches.
Foot 50 stitches.   Knit 5 inches.

Decrease in 3 rounds of the leg, 6 decreasings.

Decrease in 6 rounds of the toe, 24 decreasings.

Cast off with 26 stitches.

Ribbing.

56 *Stitches.*

Cast on 56 stitches. Knit 2, purl 2. Repeat for 3 inches (30 rounds). Knit the end of yarn into the first six stitches.

Leg.

56 *Stitches.*

On the 1st needle place 27 stitches ; 13 stitches on each side of the seam stitch. On the 2nd needle place 15 stitches. On the 3rd needle place 14 stitches. Mark the seam stitch with a loop of white cotton.

Knit the seam stitch in the 1st round; purl the seam stitch in the 2nd round. Repeat the seam stitch for the ribbing to the end of the heel. Knit 3 inches (30 rounds).

Decrease before and after the seam stitch in 3 rounds, 6 decreasings. Mark each decreasing on the right side of the seam stitch with a loop of white cotton. Decrease thus: Knit plain till there are 4 stitches before

the seam stitch, slip 1, knit 1, cross
the slip stitch over the last knitted stitch,
knit 2. SEAM STITCH. Knit 2, slip 1,
knit 1, cross the slip stitch over the last
knitted stitch, knit the rest plain. Knit
10 plain rounds between each decreasing
round.

Ankle.

50 *Stitches.*

Knit 1 inch (10 rounds). Measure from
the last decreasing round.

Heel.

25 *Stitches.*

Knit with two needles only, in rows.
Leave the 25 instep stitches on the other 2
needles. Slip the 1st stitch of each row.
Knit the 1st row, purl the 2nd row.

Knit 2 inches (20 rows).

Turn the heel thus :—Omit the seam
stitch ; mark the middle with a loop of
white cotton ; knit to the middle of the
row, knit 2, knit 2 together, knit 1.

C

Turn back. Purl to the middle of the row, purl 2, purl 2 together, purl 1. Repeat to the end of the heel.

Instep.

25 *Stitches.*

On the 1st needle take up the loops on the 1st side of the heel. On the 2nd needle place the 25 instep stitches. On the 3rd needle take up the loops on the second side of the heel. Knit 1 plain round. Knit 1 round, increasing every 3rd stitch on each side of the heel. Knit the instep stitches without increasing. Take 2 stitches from each end of the instep needle, and place them on the instep end of each heel needle. Mark the decreasings of the 1st needle with a loop of white cotton. Decrease thus :—1st needle, knit plain till 4 stitches are left on the needle, knit 2 together, knit 2. 2nd needle, knit the 25 instep stitches plain. 3rd needle, knit 2, slip 1, knit 1, cross the slip stitch over the last knitted stitch, knit the rest plain. Knit 1 plain round between each decreasing round. Decrease till there are 50 stitches on the three needles.

Foot.

50 *Stitches.*

Knit 5 inches (50 rounds). Measure from the join of the heel. Knit 1st needle plain, that the toe may begin on the upper needle.

Toe.

50 *Stitches.*

On the upper needle place 25 stitches. On the 1st under needle place 12 stitches. On the 2nd under needle place 13 stitches. Mark the 1st decreasings of the upper needle with a loop of white cotton. Decrease thus:—Upper needle, knit 2, slip 1, knit 1. Cross the slip stitch over the last knitted stitch. Knit plain till 4 stitches are left on the needle. Slip 1, knit 1. Cross the slip stitch over the last knitted stitch. Knit 2. 1st under needle, knit

2, slip 1, knit 1, cross the slip stitch
over the last knitted stitch, knit the rest
plain.   2nd under needle, knit plain till
4 stitches are left on the needle, slip 1,
knit 1, cross the slip stitch over the last
knitted stitch, knit 2.   Knit 2 plain
rounds between each decreasing round.
Decrease in 8 rounds, 24 decreasings.
Place all the under stitches on 1 needle.
Place the 2 needles together, 13 stitches on
each needle.   Cast off from both needles at
once on the right side. Darn the end of
yarn into the knitting.

To make a larger sock than the above,
use the same directions with Scotch yarn,
and No. 12 needles.   Do not measure
the inches, but count the rows of knitting.

FOURTH STAGE.

Knitting—4 needles. Girls' Stockings.

THE ANNIE STOCKING.

Balmoral Yarn. Four Needles No. 14.

Leg 68 stitches. Knit 8 inches.
Ankle 56 stitches. Knit 3 inches.
Heel 27 stitches. Knit 2 inches.
Foot 56 stitches. Knit 4 inches.

Decrease in 6 rounds of the leg, 12 decreasings.

Decrease in 5 rows of the heel, 10 decreasings.

Decrease in 8 rounds of the toe, 32 decreasings.

Cast off with 24 stitches.

Ribbing.

68 *Stitches.*

Cast on 68 stitches. Knit 2, purl 2.
Repeat for 2 inches (20 rounds). Knit
the end of yarn into the first six stitches.

Leg.

68 *Stitches.*

On the 1st needle place 23 stitches ; 11
stitches on each side of the seam stitch.
On the second needle place 23 stitches.
On the 3rd needle place 22 stitches. Knit
the seam stitch in the 1st round; purl
the seam stitch in the 2nd round. Repeat
the seam stitch from the ribbing to the
end of the heel. Mark the seam stitch
with a loop of white cotton. Knit 8 inches
(80 rounds). Decrease before and after
the seam stitch in 6 rounds, 12 decreasings.
Mark each decreasing on the right side of
the seam stitch with a loop of white cotton.
Decrease thus :—Knit plain till there are
4 stitches before the seam stitch, slip 1,
knit 1, cross the slip stitch over the last

knitted stitch, knit 2. SEAM STITCH. Knit
2, slip 1, knit 1, cross the slip stitch
over the last knitted stitch, knit the rest
plain. Knit 10 plain rounds between each
decreasing round.

Ankle.

56 *Stitches.*

Knit 3 inches (30 rounds). Measure
from the last decreasing round.

Heel.

27 *Stitches.*

Knit with 2 needles only, in rows. Leave
the 29 instep stitches on the other 2 needles.
Slip the 1st stitch of each row. Knit the
1st row, purl the 2nd row. Repeat for
two inches (20 rows). Decrease in 5 rows
on each side of the seam stitch, 10 decreasings. Mark the decreasings on the
right side of the seam stitch with a loop
of white cotton. Decrease thus:—Knit
plain till there are 4 stitches before the
seam stitch, knit 2 together, knit 2.

SEAM STITCH. Knit 2, slip 1, knit 1,
cross the slip stitch over the last knitted
stitch, knit the rest plain. Purl 1 row
between each decreasing row. After the last
decreasing row, purl to the seam stitch.
Place the two needles together. With an
extra needle, cast off from both needles at
once on the wrong side, beginning with
the seam stitch.

Instep.

29 *Stitches.*

Begin from the join of the heel. On
the 1st needle take up the loops on the 1st
side of the heel. On the 2nd needle place
the 29 instep stitches. On the 3rd needle
take up the loops on the 2nd side of the
heel. Knit 1 plain round. Knit 1 round
increasing every 3rd stitch on each side of
the heel. Knit the instep stitches without
increasing. Take 2 stitches from each end
of the instep needle and place them on the
instep end of each heel needle. Mark the
decreasings of the 1st needle with a loop of

white cotton. Decrease thus:—1st needle, knit plain till 4 stitches are left on the needle, knit 2 together, knit 2. 2nd needle, knit the 25 instep stitches plain. 3rd needle, knit 2, slip 1, knit 1, cross the slip stitch over the last knitted stitch, knit the rest plain. Knit 1 plain round between each decreasing round. Decrease till there are 56 stitches on the 3 needles.

Foot.

56 *Stitches.*

Knit 4 inches (40 rounds). Measure from the join of the heel. 1st needle, knit plain, that the toe may begin on the upper needle.

Toe.

56 *Stitches.*

On the upper needle place 28 stitches. On the 1st under needle place 14 stitches. On the 2nd under needle place 14 stitches. Mark the first decreasings of the upper needle with a loop of white cotton. Decrease thus :—Upper needle, knit 2, slip 1, knit 1, cross the slip stitch over the last knitted stitch, knit plain till 4 stitches are left on the needle, slip 1, knit 1, cross the slip stitch over the last knitted stitch, knit 2. 1st under needle, knit 2, slip 1, knit 1, cross the slip stitch over the last knitted stitch, knit the rest plain. 2nd under needle, knit plain till 4 stitches are left on the needle, slip 1, knit 1, cross the slip stitch over the last knitted stitch, knit 2. Knit 2 plain rounds between each decreasing round. Decrease in 8 rounds, 32 decreasings. Place the under stitches on one needle. Place the 2 needles together. Cast off from both needles at once on the right side. Darn the end of yarn into the knitting.

FIFTH STAGE.

Knitting—4 needles. A full-sized Boy's
Stocking.

THE STEWART STOCKING.

Scotch Yarn. Four Needles, No. 12.

Leg 76 stitches. Knit 10 inches.
Ankle 58 stitches. Knit 4 inches.
Heel 28 stitches. Knit $2\frac{1}{2}$ inches.
Foot 58 stitches. Knit 5 inches.

Decrease in 9 rounds of the leg, 18 decreasings.

Decrease in 8 rounds of the toe, 82 decreasings.

Cast off with 26 stitches.

Ribbing.

76 *Stitches.*

Cast on 76 stitches. Knit 2, purl 2. Repeat for 2 inches (20 rounds). Knit the end of yarn into the first six stitches.

Leg.

76 *Stitches.*

On the 1st needle place 27 stitches ; 13 stitches on each side of the seam stitch. On the 2nd needle place 25 stitches. On the 3rd needle place 24 stitches. Knit the seam stitch in the 1st round; purl the seam stitch in the 2nd round. Repeat the seam stitch from the ribbing to the end of the heel. Mark the seam stitch with a loop of white cotton. Knit 10 inches (100 rounds). Decrease before and after the seam stitch in 9 rounds, 18 decreasings. Mark the decreasings on the right side of the seam stitch with a loop of white cotton. Decrease thus :—Knit plain till there are · 4 stitches before the seam stitch, slip 1,

knit 1, cross the slip stitch over the last
knitted stitch, knit 2. SEAM STITCH.
Knit 2, slip 1, knit 1, cross the slip
stitch over the last knitted stitch, knit
the rest plain. Knit 10 plain rounds between each decreasing round.

Ankle.

58 Stitches.

Knit 4 inches (40 rounds). Measure
from the last decreasing round.

Heel.

28 Stitches.

Knit with 2 needles only, in rows. Leave
the 30 instep stitches on the other 2 needles.
Slip the 1st stitch of each row. Knit the
1st row ; purl the 2nd row. Repeat for $2\frac{1}{2}$
inches (26 rows). Turn the heel thus :—
Omit the seam stitch ; mark the middle
with a loop of white cotton ; knit to the
middle of the row, knit 4, slip 1, knit 1,
cross the slip stitch over it. Turn back.

Purl to the middle of the row, purl 4, purl 2 together. Repeat till the heel is finished.

Instep.

30 *Stitches*.

Begin from the join of the heel. On the 1st needle take up the loops on the 1st side of the heel. On the 2nd needle place the 30 instep stitches. On the third needle take up the loops on the 2nd side of the heel. Knit 1 plain round. Knit 1 round increasing every 3rd stitch on each side of the heel. Knit 1 plain round without increasing. Take 2 stitches from each end of the instep needle and place them on the instep end of each heel needle. Mark the decreasings of the 1st needle with a loop of white cotton. Decrease thus:—
1st needle, knit plain till 4 stitches are left on the needle, knit 2 together, knit 2. 2nd needle, knit the 26 instep stitches plain. 3rd needle, knit 2, slip 1, knit 1, cross the slip stitch over the last knitted stitch, knit the rest plain. Knit 1 plain

round between each decreasing round. Decrease till there are 58 stitches on the 3 needles.

Foot.

58 *Stitches.*

Knit 5 inches (50 rounds). Measure from the join of the heel. 1st needle, knit plain, that the toe may begin on the upper needle.

Toe.

58 *Stitches.*

On the upper needle place 29 stitches. On the 1st under needle place 15 stitches. On the 2nd under needle place 14 stitches. Mark the 1st decreasings of the upper needle with a loop of white cotton. Decrease thus:—Upper needle, knit 2, slip 1, knit 1, cross the slip stitch over the last knitted stitch, knit plain till 4 stitches are left on the needle, slip 1, knit 1, cross the slip stitch over the last knitted stitch, knit 2. 1st under needle,

knit 2, slip 1, knit 1, cross the slip
stitch over the last knitted stitch, knit
the rest plain. 2nd under needle, knit
plain till 4 stitches are left on the needle,
slip 1, knit 1, cross the slip stitch over
the last knitted stitch, knit 2. Decrease
in 8 rounds, 32 decreasings. Knit 2
plain rounds between each decreasing
round. Place the under stitches on one
needle. Place the two needles together.
Cast off from both needles at once on the
right side. Darn the end of yarn into the
knitting.

SIXTH STAGE.

Knitting—4 needles.   A long full-sized
Stocking, with Heels thickened.

THE KATIE STOCKING.

Argyle Yarn.   Four Needles, No. 14.

Cast on 84 stitches.

Ribbing, 2 inches.   Knit 2, purl 2.

Leg 11 inches plain.

Decrease in 10 rounds of the leg, 20 decreasings.

Knit 10 plain rounds between each decreasing round.

Ankle 64 stitches.   Knit 4 inches.

Heel 31 stitches.   Knit 3 inches.

Decrease in 5 rows of the heel, 10 decreasings.

D

Instep 30 stitches; decrease till instep and heel are 64 stitches.

Foot 64 stitches.   Knit 6 inches.

Decrease in 8 rounds of the toe, 32 decreasings.

Cast off with 32 stitches.

Thicken the heel thus:—Slip each alternate stitch of the heel instead of knitting it. Purl the next row as usual, or in both rows slip each alternate stitch ; or knit from two balls of yarn at once for the whole of the heel ; or, when the stocking is finished, run the whole of the heel with yarn ; or, if the stocking be of grey yarn, knit the heel with Taylor's white Persian thread No. 3 and the yarn together.

EXTRA GARMENTS
NOT SPECIFIED IN SCHEDULE III.

Infant's Comforter.

With Tassel.

Best Berlin Yarn, White.
Two Bone Needles.
Cast on 18 stitches.

Make 1, slip 1, knit 2 together. Repeat for 22 inches.

Cast off.

Gather up the stitches of the casting on and casting off, and make an inch tassel of wool by winding the wool round a book 36 times. Secure by a firm tie in two places at one end, and, an inch from the end, sew the tied end to the comforter, and cut the other end to form a tassel.

Girl's Comforter.

Chain Edge with Tassel.

Double Berlin Wool, Blue.
Two Bone Needles.
Cast on 21 stitches. Knit plain for 26 inches.

Cast off thus, very loosely:—Cast off 4 stitches, let the 5th stitch drop; cast off 6th and 7th, let the 8th drop; cast off 9th and 10th, let the 11th drop; cast off 12th and 13th, let the 14th drop; cast off the 15th and 16th, let the 17th drop; cast off the remaining 4 stitches.

Gather up the stitches of the casting on and casting off, and make an 8-inch tassel of wool by winding the wool round book 36 times. Secure by a firm tie in two places at one end and an inch from the end; sew the tied end to the comforter, and cut the other end to form a tassel.

Boy's Comforter.
Chain Edge with Fringe.

Double Berlin Wool, Scarlet.
Two Bone Needles.

Cast on 30 stitches. Knit plain for 30 inches.

Cast off.

With a bone crochet needle loop an 8-inch length of wool into each stitch of the casting on and casting off for a fringe.

'THE STANDARD GUIDE TO KNITTING.'
'THE STANDARD GUIDE TO NEEDLEWORK.'

DEDICATED BY PERMISSION TO

H.R.H. THE PRINCESS LOUISE
(MARCHIONESS OF LORNE).

The following are extracts from some few of the numerous Reviews of the above Guides.

From ' The Schoolmaster.'

'"The Guide to Knitting" is written with the object of enabling children to fulfil the requirements of that part of the Needlework Schedule which relates to knitting. The work of each standard is dealt with in turn. The directions given are full and plain, so that any child, with the help of the teacher, will be able to understand them. The "Guide to Knitting" is well calculated to answer the purpose which the writer had in view, and we cordially recommend it to the notice of our readers.'

From ' The Educational Times.'

'The series before us, dedicated by permission to the Princess Louise, is one of the best that has come under our notice. The art of the sempstress is reduced to a system, with the precision of a regimental drill-book. We have much pleasure in cordially recommending these little books.'

From ' The School Guardian.'

'Competent lady experts assure us that these Guides and diagrams are really excellent, and will be of great use to schoolmistresses in satisfying the needlework requirements of the Code.'

OPINIONS OF THE PRESS.

From 'The School Board Chronicle.'

'The authoress endeavours to lay down a self-supporting scheme, whereby the work will pay for itself. By a definite plan of teaching the task is rendered easy for the instructor, and the teaching more complete for the child. The pattern diagrams are with dimensions and minute directions.'

From the 'Illustrated London News.'

'We are certified by competent judges of the subject that these manuals are just what is wanted to set forth the rules and methods of those useful domestic arts. The little books will be equally useful in private families.'

From the 'Christian World.'

'In order to meet the requirements of the Code, "A Lady Manager" has drawn up a "Standard Guide to Needlework," which, for simplicity and clearness, is all that can be desired. Full directions for the Infants' Department and for the six standards of the Girls' Department are given, as well as carefully-drawn patterns. It is dedicated by permission to the Princess Louise. Mothers who wish to teach their little girls at home as well as schoolmistresses will value this Guide.'

From 'Church Bells.'

'"The Standard Guide to Needlework," and "The Standard Guide to Knitting" contain clear directions for teaching these subjects according to the New Code, and will prove helpful to teachers of girls' schools.'

From 'The Scottish Magazine.'

'"The Standard Guide to Needlework" contains healthy advice to teachers, with practical instructions to pupils, and accompanied by diagrams of patterns. The other is "The Standard Guide to Knitting," and is also replete with valuable details. "Our guidwife" says we may with safety recommend them heartily to the public.'